A Woman With A Herd Of Camels

FACES
AND
PLACES

SOMALIA

BY ELMA SCHEMENAUER

THE CHILD'S WORLD®, INC.

COVER PHOTO

A boy selling coconuts near Marka.
©Liba Taylor/CORBIS

Published in the United States of America by The Child's World®, Inc.
PO Box 326
Chanhassen, MN 55317-0326
800-599-READ
www.childsworld.com

Project Manager James R. Rothaus/James R. Rothaus & Associates
Designer Robert E. Bonaker/R. E. Bonaker & Associates
Contributors Mary Berendes, Dawn M. Dionne, Katherine Stevenson, Ph.D., Red Line Editorial

Library of Congress Cataloging-in-Publication Data
Schemenauer, Elma.
Somalia / by Elma Schemenauer.
p. cm.
Includes index.
ISBN 1-56766-911-5
1. Somalia—Juvenile Literature.
[1. Somalia]
I. Title.
DT401.5 .S34 2001
967.73—dc21

00-013185

Table of Contents

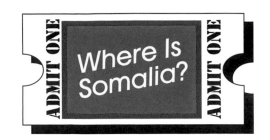
If you were soaring high above Earth, you would see huge land areas with water around them. These land areas are called **continents**. Somalia is the easternmost country on the continent of Africa. Somalia forms a large part of the "Horn of Africa," an area that juts out into the water like a rhinoceros horn.

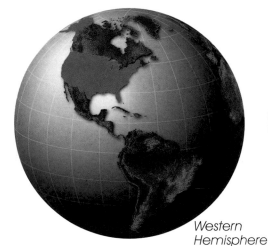

Western Hemisphere

Eastern Hemisphere

Somalia (white) is in the east and U.S.A. (green) is in the west

The Gulf of Aden lies to the north of Somalia. The Indian Ocean lies to the southeast. The three countries bordering Somalia are Djibouti (jeh-BOO-tee) to the northwest, Ethiopia to the west, and Kenya to the southwest.

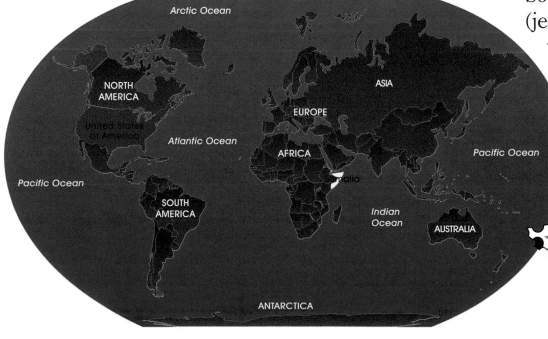

Arctic Ocean

NORTH AMERICA

United States of America

Atlantic Ocean

EUROPE

ASIA

AFRICA

Pacific Ocean

Pacific Ocean

Somalia

SOUTH AMERICA

Indian Ocean

AUSTRALIA

ANTARCTICA

The World Shown Flat

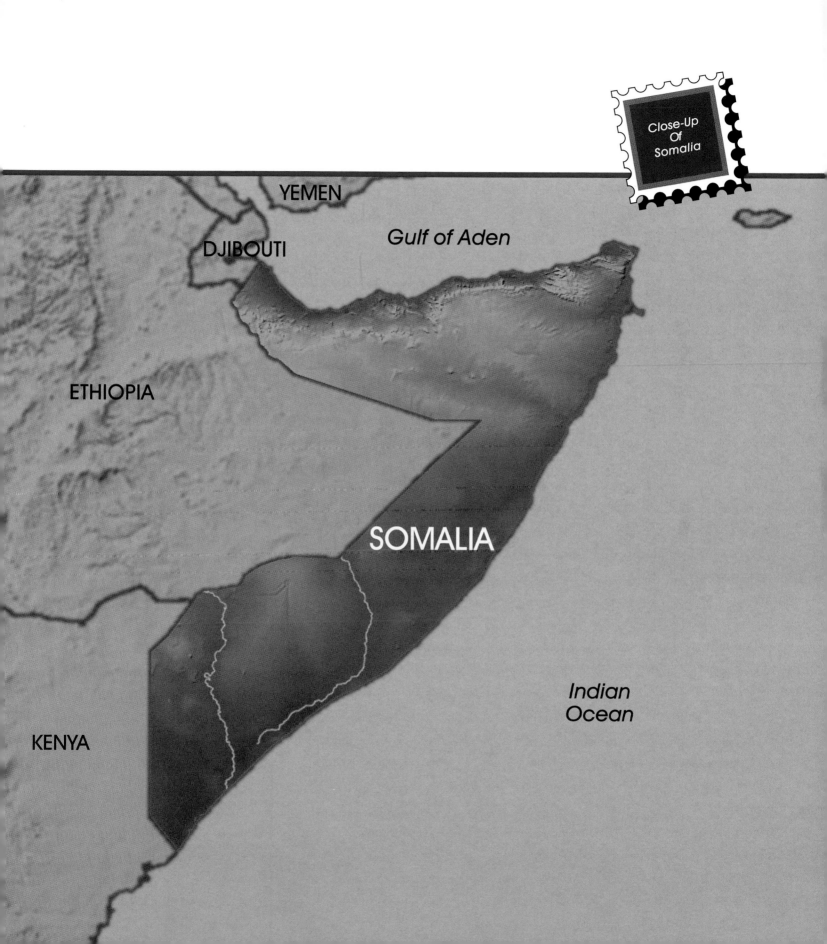

YEMEN

Gulf of Aden

DJIBOUTI

ETHIOPIA

SOMALIA

KENYA

*Indian
Ocean*

Cattle Herders
In Buur
Hakkaba

Berbera

Shabeelle
River

Jubba
River

Buur Hakkaba

Marka

©Kevin Fleming/CORBIS

The Port Of Berbera

Most of Somalia is made up of flat or rolling plains. The northern portion of the country has a narrow coastal plain with mountain ranges behind it. Somalia's southern part has two main rivers, the Jubba and the Shabeelle. They flow toward the Indian Ocean.

Wind-Sculpted Dunes Near Marka

Somalia has four seasons. December to March is a dry season. April to June is the main rainy season, when grasses and flowers burst out almost everywhere—even in the deserts. July to September is dry, and October to November usually has light rains. Even with its two rainy seasons, Somalia is a hot, dry country.

Goats
Wandering
Over A Dry
Riverbed

©Michael S. Yamashita/CORBIS

During much of the year, scattered grasses and bushes, including thorn bushes, struggle to grow on Somalia's dry plains. The plains near the Jubba and Shabeelle Rivers get a bit more rain, so the trees, bushes, and grasses grow thicker and taller there. In the northern mountains, where it is a bit cooler, some forests of junipers and other trees grow.

Shrubs
And Trees
Growing On
The Mountain
Slopes Near
Berbera

© Yann Arthus-Bertrand/CORBIS

Somalia's animals include badgers, jackals, gazelles, and antelopes. There are also a few elephants, giraffes, and zebras. Among Somalia's big cats are lions and leopards. Birds include eagles, vultures, doves, and ostriches. In Somalia, people need to watch out for poisonous snakes! These dangerous snakes include cobras, puff adders, and mambas.

2 1822 04107 1108

Berbera

Shabeelle River

Luuq

Jubba River

Camels At The Jubba River Near Luuq

Ancient Cave Markings Near Taleh

Taleh

★ Mogadishu

©Michael S. Yamashita/CORBIS

British And Arab Calvalry In The Desert In 1940

©Bettmann/CORBIS

Long ago, groups of people from several parts of Africa moved into the area now called Somalia. Arabs also arrived from Asia, bringing the religion called **Islam.** By about the year 1200, the whole area was Islamic. People raised animals, farmed, and traded. **Clans**, or groups of related families, sometimes fought over the right to use water and pasture land.

In the 1800s, Europeans arrived. Britain set up a **protectorate** in what is now northern Somalia. In return for the Somali chiefs' trade and cooperation, Britain agreed to protect them from enemy clans. South of the British protectorate, Italy set up a protectorate of its own. In time, Britain and Italy began governing the area.

©/Scheufler Collection/CORBIS

In 1960, Somalis started running their own government. The British and Italian regions joined to form one new country, Somalia.

An Italian Flag Flying Over The Governor's Palace In Mogadishu In The 1920s

Somalia Today

President Siad Barre In 1981

©Kevin Fleming/CORBIS

Several years after the new country of Somalia was formed, fighting among clans got worse after other countries gave them money for weapons. Some clans fought the government. In 1991, a group of clans drove out President Siad Barre, and the government fell apart.

The next year was very dry, so Somalia's people could not raise much food. Many people starved to death. The United Nations sent food as well as soldiers to make peace among the warring clans. But the clans fought over the food and drove out the soldiers. The last United Nations soldiers left in 1995. In 2000, a new Somali government was set up.

Leaders felt they had finally found ways to settle their problems and differences. Unfortunately, the new government still faces problems from some clan leaders and two northern areas called Somaliland and Puntland. People living in these areas want their own governments. Many people hope the new government will bring peace and order to Somalia's war-torn land.

Somalis Applauding The Arrival Of U.S. Troops In Mogadishu In 1992

©Peter Turnley/CORBIS

©David Turnley/CORBIS

SOMALILAND
PUNTLAND

★ Mogadishu

A Somali Family

A Group of Young Somali Boys Near Mogadishu

★ Mogadishu

A Somali Man Wearing A Turban In Mogadishu

The tall, slim people who make up most of Somalia's population are called Somalis. Somalis believe that they are all related, even though they are divided into several clans. Some think they came from southern Ethiopia. Others think they all descended from one Arab father and one African mother.

It is hard to be certain what happened long ago, but Somalis all share the same culture and language. Parts of their culture and language are Arabic. Other parts are African. Besides Somalis, the country also has small numbers of Italians, Arabs, Pakistanis, Indians, and Bantu-speaking peoples.

A Young Somali Woman

©Kevin Fleming/CORBIS

Nomads' Moveable Huts Near Luuq

©Kevin Fleming/CORBIS

Fewer than half of Somalia's people live in towns or cities. Many town and city dwellers live in rectangular houses with flat roofs. Some of these houses are made of stone. In big cities such as Mogadishu and Kismaayo, there are hotels, banks, restaurants, and post offices just like those in the United States.

Downtown Mogadishu

©Michael S. Yamashita/CORBIS

Many country people are **nomads** who move around to find water and pasture for their animals. Their round huts have **thatched** roofs, and walls covered with mats or animal hides. When it is time to move, the nomads take their homes apart and load them onto their camels' backs. Country people who are not nomads live in round or rectangular huts with thatched or metal roofs.

Luuq
Buur Hakkaba
Mogadishu
Kismaayo

©Kevin Fleming/CORBIS

Village Huts
Near Buur
Hakkaba

Somali Students In A Mogadishu Classroom

★Mogadishu

©David Turnley/CORBIS

The Somali government used to run free schools for children ages 6 through 14. After the government fell apart in 1991, many of its schools closed. By 1995, less than 1 in 10 children attended elementary school.

Many **Koranic schools**, however, stayed open. In these schools, children study the *Koran* (the holy book of Islam), which is written in Arabic. Some areas also have schools that are paid for by Somalis or by people from other countries who are trying to help. In the cities, wealthy families hire **tutors**, or private teachers.

Students Writing On Wood In A Koranic School

A Billboard In Mogadishu

©Michael S. Yamashita/CORBIS

©Howard Davies/CORBIS

Somali became Somalia's official national language in 1973. It is an African-Asian language. Among other languages spoken in Somalia are Arabic, Italian, English, and Bantu.

A Girl Milking A Camel

©Michael S. Yamashita/CORBIS

Sixty percent of Somalis are nomads who herd goats, sheep, camels, and cattle. Another 25 percent of the Somali people are farmers. They grow bananas, sugarcane, cotton, mangoes, corn, sesame seeds, and a corn-like plant called **sorghum**. Some Somalis also fish or do other types of work.

Somalia is a dry country with very few natural resources, so Somalis find it hard to make a living. Clan wars have made it even harder, especially since the government fell apart. Fighting has damaged the water system, which means less water for animals and crops.

Food Being Unloaded From A Ship In The Port Of Mogadishu

©Chris Rainier/CORBIS

Factories that once produced foods, cloth, and other goods have been broken down for scrap metal to make weapons. Because of the fighting, some Somalis have left the country. From their new homes in Europe, North America, and elsewhere, some send money to help needy relatives in Somalia.

Mogadishu

©Michael S. Yamashita/CORBIS

A Potter In
A Somali
Village

Women
Looking At
Fresh Bread In A
Mogadishu
Market

SOMALILAND

Hargeysa •

PUNTLAND

Shabeelle
River

★ Mogadishu

Food

For breakfast a Somali family might have rolls or flat bread with tea, or perhaps liver and onions. At noon they might eat rice or pasta with sauce, and perhaps goat or camel meat.

The evening meal is light—often flat bread or rice with salad. Somalis like milk, but they prefer milk from goats or camels rather than from cows. Other favorite drinks are coffee and tea with lots of sugar. It is against the Islamic religion to drink wine or other alcoholic drinks, or to eat pork.

A Woman Winnows Grain Near The Shabeelle River

©Liba Yaylor/CORBIS

People Selling Produce In Hargeysa

©Kevin Fleming/CORBIS

Hunger is still a problem in Somalia. Other countries send food, but clan wars often keep it from getting to the hungry. Life is a little better in Somaliland and Puntland, but food is still scarce. Leaders in all three areas are trying to work together to get enough food to everyone.

Pastimes and Holidays

Somalia is a land of poets. Somalis make up poems about God, daily life, camels, love, peace, and war. They recite their poems at events such as feasts, weddings, or blessings of new babies. They even hold contests in which poets compete to see who is the best. Somalis also enjoy music, dancing, plays, and storytelling. Some stories are about animals, and others are about long-ago heroes.

Among the yearly holidays are New Year's Day on January 1, Labor Day on May 1, and Foundation of the Republic Day on July 1. During the month of *Ramadan*, followers of Islam **fast**, or go without food, from sunrise to sunset each day.

The holiday of *Eid al Adha* celebrates the **prophet** Abraham's strong faith in God. Children love Eid al Adha because stores sell special toys and candy, and there are amusement parks where the children can play.

Somalis face many problems, including hunger, lack of water, lack of schooling, and clan wars. Yet they have not given up. A Somali proverb says, "If people come together, they can even mend a crack in the sky." Somalis hope to work toward a better future, along with other people from around the world.

Men Playing Dominoes In Mogadishu

©Kevin Fleming/CORBIS

©Kevin Fleming/CORBIS

Bosasso
Berbera
Hargeysa
Baidoa
★ Mogadishu
Marka
Kismaayo

A Somali Woman Playing A Drum In Mogadishu

Area
More than 246,000 square miles
(about 637,000 square kilometers)—a bit smaller than Texas.

Population
About 7 million people.

Capital City
Mogadishu. Somaliland, the northwestern part of Somalia, set up its
own government in 1991. Its capital is Hargeysa.

Other Important Cities
Berbera, Kismaayo, Marka, Bosasso, and Baidoa.

Money
The Somali shilling.

National Flag
The flag is light blue with a white, five-pointed star in the middle. The
blue stands for the United Nations, of which Somalia is a member. The
white color stands for peace, and the star's five points stand for
Somalia's five regions.

National Song
"Soomaaliya Ha Nolato," or "Long Live Somalia."

Official Name
The Somali Democratic Republic.

A Tribal Woman
In A Refugee
Camp

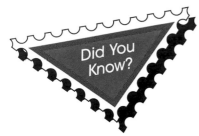

In Somalia's northern forests, some Somalis gather tree juices that harden into sweet-smelling lumps of frankincense (FRANK-in-senss) and myrrh (MURR). Frankincense is used to make incense and perfumes. Myrrh is used in perfumes and medicines.

Somali teenage boys often herd their families' camels, moving from place to place in search of water and pasture. During this time the boys' only food is camels' milk. Sometimes a hungry young camel-herder will drink 6 to 10 quarts of milk a day.

Though Somalia has no railroads, it does have some gravel and dirt roads. There is only one paved road. It runs from the port of Berbera in the northwest down to Mogadishu, and then south to Kismaayo.

People used to write the Somali language using several different alphabets. In 1974 the government decided that Somali should be written in letters like those we use for English.

	SOMALI	HOW TO SAY IT
Hello	nabad miiya	na–bat MEE–ya
Good-bye	nabad geylyo	na–bat GEL–yo
Thank You	mahadsanid	ma–HAD–sa–nit
One	kow	KO
Two	laba	LA–ba
Three	saddeh	SAD–ech
Somalia	Soomaalia	so–MAW–lee–a

clans (KLANZ)
Clans are large groups of families who consider themselves related. Clans are an important part of Somali culture.

continents (KON-tih-nents)
Most of Earth's land lies in huge land areas called continents. Somalia is on the easternmost side of the continent of Africa.

fast (FAST)
When people fast, they do not eat. During the month of Ramadan, followers of the religion of Islam fast from sunrise to sunset.

Islam (IS-lahm)
Islam is a set of beliefs about God (called Allah) and his prophet Muhammad. Many Somalis follow Islam.

Koranic schools (koh-RRAHN-ik SKOOLZ)
In Koranic schools, people study the book of Islam, called the Koran. Some Koranic schools still exist in Somalia.

nomads (NOH-madz)
Nomads are people who move from place to place rather than living in one spot. Many people in Somalia's countryside are nomads.

prophet (PRAHF-et)
A prophet is someone who speaks for God. The holiday of Eid al Adha celebrates the prophet Abraham's faith in God.

protectorate (proh-TEK-tor-et)
A protectorate provides help, goods, and cooperation to a more powerful country in return for protection from enemies. Britain set up a protectorate in northern Somalia in the 1800s.

sorghum (SOR-gum)
Sorghum is a tall plant with wide leaves that is grown in warm areas. Some Somali farmers grow sorghum, which is often used as food for farm animals.

thatched (THATCHD)
Thatched roofs are made of carefully stacked grass or straw. Many homes in Somalia's countryside have thatched roofs.

tutors (TOO-terz)
Tutors are teachers who work one-on-one with students instead of teaching an entire classroom of people. Some wealthy Somali children are taught by tutors.

Index

Web Sites

Learn more about Somalia:
http://www.arab.net/somalia/somalia_contents.html
http://lcweb2.loc.gov/frd/cs/sotoc.html
http://www.factmonster.com/ce6/world/A0845894.html
http://www.unsomalia.org/

Learn more about the struggle for peace in Somalia:
http://www.reliefweb.int/IRIN/archive/somalia.phtml

Get updated news about Somalia:
http://www.somalianews.com/